I0102110

The Stepdad's Guide

Resolving Blended Family Conflict

S. James Wheeler

All content copyright © 2012 S. James Wheeler

Cover design by Advontemedia LLC © 2012 S. James Wheeler

All rights reserved. No part of this book may be reproduced
in any form or by any electronic or mechanical means,
including information storage and retrieval systems, without
written permission from the publisher or author, except in
the case of a reviewer, who may quote brief passages
embodied in critical articles or in a review.

For my mother Dolly Wheeler—a single mom and an amazing woman

Table of Contents

Preface

This book is the culmination of several years of research which grew from a need to understand the forces at work within my marriage to a single mother. These efforts ultimately developed into the research paper *The Stepdad Dynamic.* The paper presented an emotionless look at the topic of blended family struggles. The paper defined and outlined the main challenges stepdads face in major Western countries. The research complied and presented in the original research paper eventually evolved and into this book.

The motivation for the book was my desire to broaden the information in the paper and give parents tools for overcoming the challenges inherent in step parenting. My hope is to make this information more widely available to men who are in (or about to be in) the stepdad role –and help them to increase their odds of success.

When I first began researching the topic of step-fathering, I expected to find a great deal of information on the topic. I was surprised to discover how wrong I was. An initial online search revealed that there wasn't a single information source for stepfather statistics and facts. If someone wanted information, facts and advice on being a stepdad, he had to find it one piece at a time and draw conclusions from (mostly) statistics.

Western countries are the most affected by the blended family phenomenon. The majority of people in these countries now report that they have at least one step parent in the extended family. Statistics were especially difficult to find for this group. There were many studies and findings, but they were scattered throughout dozens of websites. They only contained hard facts and not findings. A single repository for information and statistics for these countries didn't exist. I quickly realized that my research would take longer than expected. These facts had to be verified, compiled and converted to make them easy to understand. Ultimately, the process took nearly three years and the process continues as new statistics are released.

As I went through the stats I began to chronicle them and I wrote articles to share my findings –to help stepdads and blended families better understand what they were dealing with. I saw how the information had helped me in my personal life and how it had strengthened my family. I knew that if other parents understood what they were dealing with they could also overcome their challenges. Most of the statistics were from government studies and were compiled in a way that wasn't user friendly. They painted an important picture of blended family life, but were challenging to understand. I knew I needed to translate them in a user-friendly way to make them easier for parents to use. I wanted people to use the facts to improve their situation. It took some time.

While I was working on the book project I wrote articles and answered common stepdad questions. This effort to educate stepdads eventually grew into Stepdadding.com, the information and inspiration site for stepdads. The site is now viewed by stepdads on **nearly** every continent —Sorry Antarctica. We still haven't heard from you.

Questions from stepdads, bio-moms and other blended family members regularly come into our inbox at Stepdadding.com. We consistently use the compiled statistics and information as a basis for the answers. Blended family's issues aren't simple matters. However, the problems and challenges these families face are very consistent. Finding the root cause of a problem is easier than you might think.

In most blended families, knowing the problem makes it easy to suggest a cure. The real work begins when the couple applies the cure. If a couple is willing to accept the root cause then they've taken the most important step to resolving the problems it creates in their home. The issues that blended families struggle with aren't usually the true problem, but rather the effects of the actual issue. If a stepdad notices that he and his wife are having big arguments over minor issues, it's likely that the problem is actually something else.

It's natural to react to what we see and ignore what isn't obvious. This is like noticing the ripples caused by a stone tossed in the water. You don't see the sinking stone, only the effects of it. When you see ripples you might not automatically look for the cause, but you instantly notice the effect. Relationships are the same. An argument over something as basic as dirty dishes may actually have a deeper root cause. You can choose to have another argument about the symptom (the dishes) or you can identify and deal with the cause.

Many blended family couples are surprised to hear how simple it is to understand the root cause of their problems. That's a natural reaction. You may have been struggling to understand your relationship challenges for some time. It seems silly to think that someone who isn't in the relationship might be able to shed some light. It's not as magical as it sounds. The dynamics created in these families can be modeled and understood.

At the core of this book are The Blended Family Conflict Models.™ These models will help couples to understand the forces that drive conflict in their marriage. There are several conflict models and each family model faces different challenges. It's important to remember that these challenges are in addition to those of a normal married couple. These include: money problems, personality conflicts, work related stress, bad habits & sexual incapability. Combined with normal marriage stress, these challenges can feel overwhelming to blended family couples. This accounts for the extremely high divorce rate in stepfamilies.

The models are consistent and even somewhat predictable. They are so consistent that you can easily track the expected divorce rate based on the family model. As dire as this might sound, they can also be used to understand the family dynamics and to save your marriage. Understanding what's broken is the first step. Commitment by the couple to do what it takes to fix it is the final step.

My goal in publishing this research and outlining the Blended Family Conflict Models™ is to help struggling couples succeed. By understanding the principles presented in this book you can improve the happiness in your home. By applying these principles you can greatly increase your odds of staying together.

Introduction

The purpose of *The Stepdad's Guide* is to define the subject and the challenges of being a stepfather in most Western cultures. The turmoil that grows from step fathering is rooted as a social issue and defined by conflict. For simplicity, this challenging dynamic will be referred to as the dynamic. The target audience for this compiled research is men who are stepfathers, or are about to become stepfathers.

Due to the target audience, we will focus exclusively on factors that affect this group. Step mothers and single mothers who marry will face similar challenges to those mentioned here. These challenges reflect the other half of the dynamic we'll be examining. The fact that we will not be dealing with half of the dynamic should not be seen as a denial that it exists—only that it is not our focus here. The intention of this research is to define and explain the primary issue—in the belief that understanding a problem is the first step to resolving it. Understanding this dynamic will help men to overcome the challenges involved with being a stepfather and to adjust to deal with these issues.

The dynamic is not created instantly when man marries a single mom. All of the necessary elements are there and the dynamic evolves over time from the effect of these elements. This can be thought of as seeds that will only grow when the right conditions are present. The marriage of the stepdad to the single mom creates a family environment with fertile conditions for the dynamic to grow. Because personalities are involved, the dynamic varies from couple to couple, but most of the root causes are the same for each couple.

The root causes may include:

- Pre-existing or conflicting rules
- The ex-husband and ex in-laws
- Children's ages
- Parenting styles
- The stepdad in the punisher role
- Resistance to change (by anyone in the family)
- Kid's genders/personalities
- Mom's unspoken expectations of stepdad
- Stepdad's assumptions about the role he will play

The root causes create ripples on the tranquil waters of the home and ultimately result in larger waves of discontent. The longer a couple is together, the more blurry the root causes become until they lose sight of the cause and begin to only see the effect. The turmoil usually continues to grow until the problem becomes overwhelming and creates a vital need to find a resolution and create a happier home life. However, it's not simple.

The resolution process takes patience and skill. The problem is like a leaking dam. When a dam is leaking you can chose to simply patch the spot where the water is escaping. However, this will not change the fact that there is a crack in the dam. The leak is not the problem but a symptom of the actual problem. To truly fix the problem you need to identify the source of the leak—which is the actual problem. Once the source of the problem is identified then you are able to repair it. Taking care of the true problem prevents a re-occurrence of the symptom—and potentially avoids a complete failure of the dam itself.

In a relationship—like the dam—you can react to the symptom, or identify and work on the true issue. Unfortunately, people rarely take time to explore and find the true issue. Instead they put their energies into the symptom. Finding and working on the source of the problem is much more challenging and takes more effort. Like the water leak in the dam, the symptom is easy to identify and generally the first thing we notice. We patch the leak in the dam, but because this doesn't fix the problem. As a result, our efforts have short-lived benefits. Dealing with the actual problem has longer lasting benefits and is the only way to truly fix what is broken. This handbook will define the issue of the stepdad disadvantage, provide evidence of its existence and make recommendations on how to overcome the problem.

Identifying the issues involved with the stepdad disadvantage can make a huge difference to those who have married single moms –or are preparing to marry one. It isn't generally recognized as a societal problem or acknowledged as a problem in step-family relationships. As a result, many couples suffer through their marriage without understanding the root causes of their turmoil. For many people, their relationship can be like a closet. They can see more clearly what's inside when they step back from them. Therefore, the dynamic usually isn't identified by a couple as a major issue while they are in the early stages of their relationship. It is usually found while in the process of marriage counseling or (more typically) it becomes clear after a divorce.

It is vital for men to understand that the stepdad disadvantage is a mainstream issue. It affects almost all stepfathers. Understanding this will help men who marry single mothers to be better prepared to deal with the uncomfortable dynamic they'll find themselves in. If they don't understand what's ahead, then they will be caught off guard by the sudden realities of step-fatherhood. Like driving a car if you know how the road will bend ahead, then you won't be caught off guard when there's a hair-pin turn. Without a map or an understanding of what to expect—surprises can have a very bad affect. Knowing about the turns in the road can save lives. Knowing about the twists in the stepdad relationship can save marriages.

Understanding the Dynamic

Defined: The Stepdad Disadvantage is created by a group of conditions existing within a stepfather's family relationship. These conditions can exist whether or not he brings children of his own into the marriage. These conditions work against his efforts to be an effective father figure to his step children and damage the strength of his relationship with his wife. The stress created by this negative dynamic, results in a higher probability of divorce than success.

Evidence: According to statistics from the governments of the US, the UK and Canada, the percentage of second marriages ending in divorce ranges from 68% to 73% when step children are a part of the family. These results show that about 7 out of every 10 marriages involving blended families will fail. The same studies demonstrate failure also comes at a faster rate than traditional first marriages.

Accepted norms, customs & traditions: In Western culture –and especially English speaking countries (including the US, UK, Canada, Australia, Ireland and others), the accepted norm for how a family is defined has evolved over time. However, in the mind of the majority, family still means a mother, father and child—or children, (and/or the extended family of a mother and father). Within this understanding of accepted norms, there is an acceptance in society that parents have certain traditional roles to fill. These are based on historical gender roles. Though these roles can vary (based on the attitudes of each parent couple and continue to evolve as societies evolve), there are underlying roles that sociologists acknowledge are still embedded in us. These are underlined by common parental functions, which have been widely accepted through history and cultures:

1) Mothers are nurturing and are role models for their female children.
2) Fathers are disciplinarians and role models for their male children.
3) Both play protective roles; the mother for the children; the father for the entire family.

These roles have existed since the beginning of recorded history and are almost entirely consistent from one culture to another. It is easy to argue that these roles are part of a common evolution of the human species. Though the thousands of years of recorded history may seem like a long time to people whose lives average about 77 years; 3000 years is not even a blink in the evolutionary process. True change takes much longer.

The nurturing mother role is so strong it can be seen throughout the entire animal kingdom; with few exceptions. Where a mother is not nurturing –she stands out as abnormal. One example frequently given that mothering isn't instinctual is the Emperor Penguin, which was featured in the 2005 film *March of the Penguins.* This penguin is used as an example because the male hatches the egg rather than the female. The example neglects the important fact that once the chick is hatched the mother becomes solely responsible for it. Mothers seem to nurture by instinct. Though not all human mothers nurture, most do. Like the animal kingdom, those who neglect their young are generally considered abnormal by society.

Within the last 50 years, society has evolved and changed. This change has slowly altered the accepted roles of mother and father in relationships in the Western cultures. What was once the standard and accepted norm in Western societies is now optional in many cases.

It was once uncommon for:

- A woman to work
- A father to be a stay-at-home dad
- A wife to make more money than her husband

These family situations are now commonly accepted in most (if not all) of Western society. The roles we once considered traditional are now hidden beneath the changes we've seen in our households and workplaces. The traditional roles now seem 'old fashioned' for many people. As time goes on, we are more likely to see these roles portrayed in old black and white TV shows than in the modern family. As a result, people don't think much about it— and some might even assume that the traditional roles are extinct. But they are not. They are alive and living well beneath the surface of the modern family.

We tend to disregard what we don't see, but it doesn't make something less true because we don't see it. We don't see oxygen or gravity either, but we still see their effects. In most modern families, the traditional roles are well out of sight. However, they continue to be at the foundation of our societies and we still see their effects. The world has changed. It's no longer unusual to have a woman as your manager at work. Men are no longer most likely to be the only breadwinner in their home. Women can speak their minds freely without feeling like they are over-stepping boundaries. These changes have some positive results, but they also have some trade-offs. As the roles shift, expectations of specific behaviors also become unclear to some men and women. This uncertainty can become a heavy burden for stepdads whose roles are not clearly defined by their wives—or well-defined to their new kids.

Accepted Norms and Stepdads

The word "dynamic" is defined as "pertaining to or characterized by energy or effective action" The stepdad dynamic is actually an 'anti-dynamic'. It is characterized by barriers which block energy or effective action. At the roots of this anti-dynamic are the traditional roles, which were created by several thousand years of family traditions in our societies. We may have evolved and grown away from those roots, but they are still firmly at the foundation of the Western family. They work against a stepdad's efforts to be effective in his role. The blended family easily becomes the perfect environment for the stepdad dynamic to grow.

As stated earlier, a biological mother will commonly take on the role of nurturer and protector of her children. Biological fathers tend to take on the role of disciplinarian and role model for their sons. They also generally have a protective nature towards their family. In a traditional family, this dynamic has evolved to work well as a standard. It allows the family to function as each person more-or-less accepts a role without questioning it. It's natural for personalities and desires to vary a bit, so the system is not perfect. However, it has worked well enough to become the accepted norm throughout history and across cultures.

The strength of this accepted norm is so embedded in us that a stepdad joining a new family will frequently (if not most of the time) assume the role of traditional father. He will often do this without even considering a need to announce his intentions. He and the mother may not have even spoken about it before they married. Because of the accepted norm, it is natural for a man to assume the role without making the choice, but rather by impulse. Men who don't assume this role usually make a conscious choice not to. The new stepdad will usually act as he believes a father should act. This may start as bonding activities with the children, but as he continues, he may start to lend a hand in role-modeling for the male children and correcting the children's behaviors. As he continues to define his role by his actions, he may find that he encounters roadblocks.

Common roadblocks
- The mother questions his use of discipline.
- The biological father has a jealous (or territorial) reaction to his children's relationship with their stepdad.

- The children resist bonding efforts or don't recognize the stepdad as an authority figure in their home.
- The mother's defensive behavior about the children makes him question his standing in the family.
- Two separate standards of acceptable behavior emerge for the kids, which the children can interpret as the stepdad being a mean guy and the mom being nice.

Ultimately, the rules and expectations can seem undefined to the stepdad. The kids can also become confused and annoyed because they have to deal with a set of double standards, created by two parents who aren't working from the same set of rules. These end results (which grow from accepted norms) work against the stepdad's ability to be an effective parent and a contented husband.

The effect of accepted norms:

1) The mother's instinct to protect her child, works against the stepdad's desire to fill the traditional father role and help the child develop into a good adult.
2) The biological father's fear of being replaced by another man leads to sometimes irrational and obstructionist behavior, which can block the stepdad's effort to bond with the child and alienate the child against his mother.
3) The children mirror the attitudes of their mother and biological father and refuse to accept the stepdad's authority in the home.
4) The children push back on the stepfather's efforts to bond with them and to be an authority figure in the home.

5) The stepdad becomes disenchanted with the situation and contemplates divorce.

If the stepdad decides to stay, he finds himself in a position where he has to redefine what his role is, based on what his wife's reactions to his behaviors are. If he gets push back from his step-children he might also adjust the way he approaches his relationship with them, based on how they react to him and how the mother has reacted to him in a father role. This diminished role can result in a more lax household and less disciplined or well-behaved kids. This situation has the potential to create new, unhealthy standards in the minds of the children. Based on their mother's actions, it is acceptable to have a man in the home—who has little authority over the family. This odd family dynamic becomes a new acceptable norm for the kids, which they might mirror later in life.

The stepdad becomes frustrated by the level of difficulty involved with what he thought would be a more manageable situation. He has struggled to be a good father figure—only to find his wife doesn't appreciate his efforts. As he struggles to define his role and the family members resist, he will start to feel isolated. He may become discouraged and begin to withdraw. The kids and wife aren't happy with him and he starts to feel like he is becoming the common enemy of the rest of the family. They rally around each other and he begins to feel like an outsider.

If the stepdad reaches the point of feeling that he has no ability to exhibit authority over the kids because his role in the home has been minimized, he will generally search for options to resolve the issue of the family dynamic.

The Most Common Choices Available for a Stepdad in Turmoil:

1. Accept the situation and find a way to deal with the frustration he feels

This is an attractive option because it allows the stepdad to avoid rocking the boat with his wife. It seems like an easy choice, but very few people have the ability to completely ignore something they find frustrating. Human nature will win out over his best intentions. This is like the sound of a dental drill. You can tolerate it because you have to, but at some point it begins to erode your nerves. Choosing this solution will give you a temporary break from the actual problem, but will not fix the underlying issue.

2. Adjust his mind-set and behavior with the kids so he takes on the role of something closer to an uncle figure, rather than a father figure—leaving discipline to the mother

Changing the way he approaches the kids and the role he plays also seems like a simple alternative. It might be a way to make everyone happy. The kids won't have to worry about him being Mr. Meanie-Pants and the wife can stop telling him to lighten up on the kids. Don't be fooled. This option is destined for failure. His wife will quickly feel abandoned and she will feel like she is now carrying the weight of a lone parent. She's felt that before –before you arrived– and she won't appreciate feeling it again. Despite what her earlier actions might have indicated, she married you because she wanted a partner. This includes her desire to have help with the kids.

3. Decide that the relationship is not
   working and choose to leave the
   marriage

This option is the equivalent of running a
white flag up the mast and admitting
defeat. You took on more than you thought
you could handle and now you're going to
walk away from it. The unfortunate truth is
2/3 (or more) of stepdads * ultimately sign
divorce papers. Those who make it to ten
years are the exception. The majority will
fail. Many marriages can be saved by using
the tools in this book, but there is no
denying that many men aren't cut out to be
stepdads. Those who aren't equipped to
handle the stress levels and challenges
won't have a very positive influence on
their new family. Men who intend to marry
a single mom should have a true
understanding of what they are about to
take on before they marry. If a man who

has married a single mom truly believes he's not up to the challenge, he should walk away. Staying and being a bad father is more emotionally destructive to kids than the effects of losing a father figure. If he is struggling, but wants to stay and find a way to fix it—there is one more option.

4. Accept that something is broken and commit to improving the marriage and family life

This option will require a complete commitment from the husband and wife. This could be a painful process, depending on how much work needs to be done. The longer a couple is in a relationship, the more that relationship has evolved. What may have been unthinkable at the start of the relationship slowly becomes an accepted norm. A stepdad might have no tolerance for a child who treats her mother with disrespect, but over time he might force himself to ignore it if his wife continually tells him "Don't worry about it. I'll deal with it." But a pattern of behavior rarely fixes itself—and patterns will continue until they are forced to change. If the mother doesn't force the change in behavior, then it becomes an accepted norm and the stepdad pretends to ignore the fact that the kid is out of control.

Accepted norms in a family can build up over time. The stepdad may adopt a detached attitude about the kids in an effort to not allow the situation to frustrate him. The mother may see his detachment as a lack of interest in her needs or an unwillingness to be helpful. Animosity can build between them as neither completely understands the other's actions or reactions to the issue. The longer they are together, the more their relationship builds on these eroding foundations.

At the center of healing the family is the need to heal the relationship. If mom and dad work, then it's easier to make the rest of the situation work. If you've been together a short time it will be easier because you've had less time to develop bad habits. The longer a couple waits to address the issues, the more challenging it becomes. If it's been a longer relationship you will have to peel back the layers to better understand the dynamic that has evolved. This can be challenging and painful—and could require the help of a marriage counselor.

Should the stepdad choose to stay and work to improve the relationship with his wife and family, he will need the proper tools -to have any hope of success. Understanding the dynamic at work and having his wife fully acknowledge the dynamic is vital. Without this, his efforts to improve the situation will have only short-lived results. Working on a relationship alone is like playing tennis alone. It starts fast and is over quickly.

*The divorce rate for stepdads can be as high as 73%, depending on the country you are in and the Blended Family Conflict Model™ you are in.

Additional variables

Men also encounter other variables within the stepdad disadvantage scenario. The complete list of potential variables is too large to fully define. The variables are diverse because individual personalities play a large part in how things develop in each relationship. Because of this factor, many of the possible variables don't exist in the average relationship and, for this reason are not worth trying to list here. These examples represent the variables stepdads are most likely to encounter in their relationships:

1) **Joining a family already in progress:** One of the biggest challenges in being a stepfather is entering a family where ground rules and expectations are already in place. As we've established, moms tend to be more nurturing than

dads are, and are much more likely to allow themselves to bend to the will of the kids in an effort to make the kids happy. Many moms believe that happy kids are a sign that they are a good mom. Men, in the traditional disciplinarian role, are traditionally the sterner of the two parents. In families where there is a mom and a dad from the beginning, there is a consistency in the way the kids are raised. In a situation where the kids have a single parent for an extended period, there is one standard they have followed and become used to. When a new father figure enters this situation, it's normal for kids to be unresponsive or resistant to the change. It's also natural for a stepdad to not be tolerant of a child who seems to be out of control. Many stepdads complain of feeling like an outsider in their own homes.

2) **The extended family:** Step children frequently have their biological father's side of the family in their lives, even after their mother and biological father split up. These relationships will likely continue for the children's entire lives, so the stepdad will have times where he will likely be in contact with this group of people. There can be occasions where there are conflicts over who the children spend their holidays, birthdays and vacation periods with. Stepdads often find themselves spectators to the turmoil –if not unwilling participants; as they take on the role of their wife's protector. Many stepdads don't consider this matter before marrying a single mom.

3) **Children's age groups**: Depending on the age of a child (and many other factors), he or she is more or less likely to be accepting of a new father figure. If a man marries a woman with children who are over the age of 11, he will likely find it much harder to bond or be able to easily create a position of authority in the home without alienating the children. Younger children —and especially the very young (4 and younger) are much more open to bonding; though they may be less open if they still have their bio fathers actively in their lives.

4) **Blending two groups of children**: When children from the wife and the husband are blended to create a new family unit, problems are bound to occur. Just as accepted norms have affected the relationships; accepted

norms in one family vary from the accepted norms in another. Simple matters like bedtimes, school grade expectations, meal times, accepted manners, phone use and personal hygiene can become points of discussion between parents. Dealing with these topics leads to animosity from the kids, as they are forced to change to create a single standard in the home. Petty jealousy can become a common issue as parents play favorites or over-compensate in an effort to not appear to be playing favorites. "Dad, why do her kids get to _____ but I don't?" and other similar phrases can become common. The Brady Bunch was a successful show about a blended family but it wasn't realistic about the issues that blended families face. The kids always listened to and respected both parents. No one said "You're not my dad" and everything at the Brady house ran smoother than most homes in America.

5) **The Stepdad's Interaction with Male Step Children:** This is a challenging relationship. The older the step-son, the more challenging the dynamic. If the mother has raised the boy for an extended period of time with little to no male oversight, the boy will probably push back on the idea of another male in the house—and will especially oppose another male having any authority over him. Mothers are likely to nurture and the boy is likely to take advantage of her easy nature. Mothers are often quick to give what their children desire to make them happy, sometimes feeling

that a happy child means good parenting. Like adults, children like to get a "yes" much more than a "no". When a child becomes used to constant yeses they will react badly when things suddenly change. For those who have ever seen the Comedy Central program South Park, the character Eric Cartman is a good example of a child coddled by a single mother to the extreme. We laugh, not just because it's funny but because we've all know someone like Cartman.

Simple Solutions to the Problems Encountered in Stepdad Relationships

Despite the name of this chapter, the reality is there is only one simple solution to the stepdad dynamic. Sadly, most single mom/stepdad couples end up taking this solution. The simple solution is divorce, but there is only one solution that gives a potential stepdad a zero percent chance of divorce.

1. **Don't marry a single mother.** This is the ultimate preventive measure. This is sort of like people who are miserable when they sunburn, and who don't like sand in their laundry avoiding the beach. The majority of all-day visits to the beach will net one or both of these results. If these are a reasonable price to pay, then it's not an issue. If, however, you loathe sand in your

laundry or have a family history of skin cancer, then it might not be worth the risk. The same is true with marrying a single mom. Are you okay with the potential for divorce? Will you mind if you lose the kids that you've grown attached to? How much is acceptable? If you can't imagine ever being OK with the likely result, then this is the best option for you.

If you truly want to make it work, there is a solution but only if a man and his wife is willing to commit to do the work. **If he is alone in his commitment, then there is no point in trying to improve the dynamic**. Without cooperation and commitment from both people in the marriage, any efforts to improve the situation will fail. Of the two, she will naturally have a higher level of respect from her children. If he hopes to gain their respect he will need her support to achieve that goal. She must be willing to be uncomfortable for a while as she re-trains the kids. This will be a lengthy process and will require her to teach by example.

Many stepfathers' marriages will end while they struggle to make it work. People are resistant to change. Single moms are no different than the rest of us. Adjusting the dynamic will require moms to make an uncomfortable change in the way things are done. Many will resist the change. As a result, many marriages will fail. If nothing changes then the odds of success remain around 28%, but the odds can be greatly improved if the changes are implemented before marriage.

2. **Decide beforehand what the rules are.** This also is a preventive measure. If you haven't married but are planning to marry a single mom, put in the work now and save the frustration later. Have a meeting and go over every little thing you can consider that might be a point of contention with the kids. You won't be able to talk about every possible scenario because there are too many variables to imagine, but you can at least deal with the most likely issues.

Decide on what your expectation levels will be for:
- Homework
- Chores
- Bed times
- Behavior
- Dating

- Computer use
- Cell phone use
- Snack rules and any other issues that come to mind.

The more issues that you consider the better it is. Along with the expectations that you agree on, also discuss what punishments you feel are fair for breaking rules. Write everything down as you go. This will give you the opportunity to talk more about them—and to make sure that you are both in agreement. When writing it out, be consistent about the application of expectations and punishment. Being consistent with kids is the most effective way to keep them heading in the right direction. Kids will be quick to take advantage of gray areas in your household law.

Clearly spell out the rules to the kids—especially if these are rules not already in place. Expect some pushback on the new rules if the kids are teens or tweens. New rules will immediately be seen as the stepdad's "fault" by the kids. For this reason, don't make a rule just for the sake of making them. Make sure there's a good reason.

A vitally important point: It is best if the mom does the punishing. Making the stepdad the enforcer will make him the bad guy in the kid's eyes and make bonding with them challenging—if not impossible. If mom is punishing them they will get over it. If the stepdad is the enforcer, then you are setting yourself up for almost certain failure. Think about it: If someone came into your house and said you had to do something a certain way you'd be resistant too. This is exactly how the kids see it. It's their house—and that's exactly as they should see it. Their feeling of possession means they are comfortable there... and that's what you want.

Conflict Models

The Blended Family Conflict Models (BFCMs) were developed over a period of several years. Each model includes challenges specific to each individual marriage situation as well as the odds of success or failure. To anticipate the challenge you can expect in your marriage, find the model that most-closely represents your situation. Bear in mind that your model may evolve as you are married. The BFCMs are not static. They change as your family situation evolves.

If you marry a woman with an ex-spouse who is not involved—there is a good likelihood he may someday become involved. If he does, then his presence will change the conflict model you are in- and will increase the challenges that you will have to deal with. If you and your wife decide to have more children, this will also change the model you are in and you can expect new challenges associated with that change. Take a moment to consider these factors as you plan for the future. You might be comfortable with how things are now, but what if things change?

Classic Nuclear Family Model: Two parents and their children

In this traditional model, the couples face typical domestic and family issues. Since complications are mainly based on the personality, the two adults need to work well together to succeed as a couple. **With this model, they will have a divorce rate of about 46%.** Only slightly more will succeed than fail.

Marriage to a Single Mom: Man with no kids marries single mom

This model depicts a situation where the single man with no children marries a single mother. The father of the children is not a part of their lives (as in the case of abandonment, incarceration or death of the father). This situation also relies on only two personalities to succeed or fail -but it faces greater challenges than a traditional marriage.

Additional Challenges

- Communication: Being able to talk, plan and strategize becomes more important for success. Agreements should be made and kept about what the stepdad's parenting role will be.

- Kid resistance: The older the children are, the more resistant they may be towards the stepdad's authority.
- Extended family: Paternal grandparents, aunts and uncles may be involved in the kid's lives. Depending on how they regard you, it can create a challenging situation. Some grandparents can be hostile towards a new man taking on their son's role with their grandchildren.

In this model, divorce rates rise above the 50% mark and failure becomes more likely than success.

Marriage to Single Mom with Ex-spouse:
Ex-spouse actively involved in kid's life

In this model, the children's father is still involved in their lives. It is similar in its dynamic to the reverse situation; where a single dad with an ex-spouse marries a woman with no children. This situation is increasingly challenging because there is an additional personality involved in the relationship that a man will have with his step children.

Additional Challenges

- <u>Legal and financial challenges</u>: The ex-spouse dynamic can involve financial and legal challenges which create high levels of stress in the couple's personal relationship.

- The ex: He now becomes a constantly present third party to the relationship and will probably be there in some form as long as a stepdad is married to his wife.
- Bonding challenges: Biological fathers can demonstrate jealous and territorial behaviors over their children. Some will even talk openly about their feelings towards the step father or ex-spouse. This behavior can confuse the children and even turn their kids against a stepdad, making it hard to create a bond with them.
- Communication challenges: The ability to work together as a team now becomes vital -since an ex-spouse can have a great deal of influence on your life –even if you never interact with them. A stepdad and his wife will need to be in agreement about how to handle any number of issues that could be created by the biological father. These issues are so varied it is nearly impossible to be prepared for all of them.

In this model the divorce rate is into the 60% range.

True Blended Family: Both parents bring kids

into the marriage

The blended family model represents two
divorced parents getting married
and bringing their kids together to create
a blended family. This dynamic can be twice as
much work and twice as much
stress as the 'marriage to a single mom'
model listed above. There are now two ex-
spouses and the children are shared among these
two sets of parents.

Additional Challenges

- <u>Twice as many disagreements with the other biological parent</u>: Custody/legal issues, disagreements over diet, grade expectations, bed times, visitation days (and more).

- <u>Double the arguments</u>: Questions over who the children spend the holidays with, when they are to be picked up and dropped off, what rules they are expected to follow while at the other parents' houses, grade and diet expectations.

- <u>Creating a family unit</u>: Perceived favoritism can create jealousy and animosity between the kids and the couple. Trying to bond with the step kids can be misperceived by biological kids as favoritism.

In this model the divorce rate is around the 65% range

Extended-Blended Family (EBF) Model: Parents divorce, remarry and have more kids

The extended family model creates a situation where kids will have half-siblings—creating an increasingly challenging dynamic. This model may also include new children the couple has together.

This dynamic continues to be -not only- hard to manage but also more emotionally destructive to the children in the family —as they struggle to define their individual places in the family. Many kids experience devastating emotional effects. These can be long-term. These effects only add to the challenges that stepdads already face. Shanon, a 25 year old mother of three, relates how she still feels, many years after being a stepdaughter with a half-sister. "...favoritism was played and my sister was my dad's baby. She could do no wrong and there was a noticeable distinction in the way I was treated when compared to that of my sister. ...I didn't feel like I measured up and was accepted. I was just something that came with the (marriage) package." These perceptions by a child (whether real or imagined) can be hard for a stepdad to overcome and can be a destructive force in a marriage relationship, as you try to sort out the issue and help the child.

About seven out of every 10 couples will split up when they marry into this type of dynamic.

Solutions to the Issue

As we discussed earlier, there are some pre-emptive things a stepdad can do to improve his odds of avoiding divorce from a single mom. The big solution is to realistically approach the issue and actively work to improve it. There is only **one** complete solution to the challenges of this family dynamic.

A Complete Solution to the Stepdad Disadvantage

Acknowledge the dynamic exists within your relationship and work as a couple to fix it:

Changing the dynamic requires both people in the relationship to first acknowledge that the dynamic exists and agree that it has a negative influence, which keeps them from becoming stronger as a couple and a family. If this cannot be agreed upon, then there is no reason to try to change the dynamic. Your efforts will be wasted since this is a team effort. Working to truly change the dynamic is like playing teeter-totter, or having a game of tug-of-war—it truly can't be done alone. If you do get buy in from your spouse, take the time to agree that the most important reason to fix the dynamic is to improve the children's home life. All the work that you do here should be with the children's best interest at the heart of it.

Set the right scene and tone:
Before you can begin you need the right environment. In the best case, this exercise will be done away from the home in a private and relaxing place. This could be a hotel room

overlooking the ocean if the budget allows or on a beach, if budget is tight but the weather allows. This exercise can only be started if you are both eager to fix what is broken with an open mind and without trying to attach blame. This exercise is not about blame but about identifying and changing behavior that works against the goal.

Before you begin, there should be specific issues or challenges that you'd like to overcome. Consider the issue of the children's attitude towards their stepdad as an example. If they don't seem to like, or respect their stepdad, this may not be about the kids, (and usually isn't) but about an outside influence. It is very common, for instance, for children to react to their biological father's attitude about their mother's re-marriage. You'll need to identify where the root of the problem is by first identifying the issue and working backwards.

1) **Define the main characters who have a role in the dynamic**
   a. The biological father
   b. The wife
   c. The stepdad
   d. The kids

2) **Define more precisely the negatives each of the characters is bringing to the relationship to create the dynamic. Factors might include:**

   a. **The biological father:**
      1. Influence on the relationship
      2. Influence on the kid's behavior
   b. **The mother:**
      1. Her desire to protect the children

      2. Her desire to keep things in
         the home the same as they
         were before the marriage

c. **The stepdad:**
  1. His impulse to be a father figure
  2. His desire to be the head of the household
  3. His need to make things work
  4. His emotional response to being treated differently than he feels he deserves

d. **The kids:**
  a. Acting out
  b. Working against the parent(s)
  c. Being belligerent towards the stepdad or mother
  (Please note: The parents are the actual root of the dynamic. Issues with children are only a symptom, but are included on this list as a means of defining the effects of the negative family dynamic)

3) **Drill down and AGREE that these issues you identify are indeed causing problems.**

   Identifying and agreeing are a vital step. If you can't agree, you are not united and will not be able to negotiate in good faith about changing the situation. If one of you feels pushed to agree, then stop and take a time out. Back up and re-approach the issue. You may agree now, in order to keep the peace, but in the end you are actually wasting time if you don't actually agree with your spouse about the issue. This process can be emotionally charged and may leave one or both of you feeling judged or attacked. Be sure to talk it out respectfully. If you can't agree, move on to the next subject.

Examples of possible topics:
   a. **The biological father:**
      1. Influence on the relationship

- Is he doing specific things which have a ripple effect in your home life?
- Is he being demanding in matters about the kids?

2. Influence on the kid's behavior
    - Is he alienating the children against the mother or you?
    - Does he demand that the kids not treat you like—or call you "dad"?
    - Does he demand to see the kids whenever he wants, despite visitation or custody agreements?
    - Does he respect and support the kid's homework schedule on the days that he has them?

b. The mother:

1. Her desire to protect the children
   - Does she disagree with the stepdad in front of the kids?
   - Does she undermine him in other ways—such as: Countermanding a punishment or letting them off easy after a punishment has been handed down. Does she say "yes" to the kids after he's already said "no"?

2. Her desire to keep things in the home the same as they were before the marriage
   - Do rules seem fixed and non-negotiable?
   - Is she not willing to accept help from you?
   - Do her actions make you confused about what her expectations of you are?

c. The stepdad:

1. His impulse to be a father figure
   - Is he trying too hard?
   - Do the kids seem to be pulling away?
   - Does he try to discipline or speak to the kids when they misbehave, only to have it backfire on him?
2. His desire to be the head of the household
   - Does he act the role of husband and father but feels she doesn't like it or she doesn't understand him?
3. His need to make things work
   - Is he acting in certain ways in order to get along, different from how he normally acts? Is that confusing her?
   - Does he feel like he is letting her make most of the decisions because it's easier than trying to force his will on the situation?

Once the issues are identified, brainstorm the items on your list in each category to overcome the issue. Negotiate a solution.

Example:
1) She disagrees with you in front of the kids. Tell her you understand she loves and wants to protect the kids. You care about them and want to protect them too. As part of that protecting, ask her to agree to a simple rule that you both agree never to argue or discuss the kids within their hearing range.
2) He plays the role of father and insists on choosing the punishment. Tell him how you feel about it and suggest a different way to approach the punishment issue.
3) She doesn't allow you to discipline the kids. Agree that it's best if you aren't the punisher, but ask her to agree to start including you in the deciding process about what's to be done with them when the kids

misbehave. She married you because she loves you, so she should respect you enough to at least listen to your opinion.

4) The biological father talks negatively about the mom in front of the kids. Agree that she should speak diplomatically about it and explain how it's making the kids confused, distracted and sad. Ask him for a cease-fire. If this doesn't fix the issue, go back to the table and consider other ways to deal with the matter (possibly legal options).

5) Her teen son talks disrespectfully to her. Explain that you can't allow the behavior to continue because it's not acceptable for a child to treat his mother that way. Talk about why he does it and look for a solution to the matter. Any changes to what the expectations are with the kids should be explained by her to them- not by the stepdad.

These agreements should be written down and agreed to. You can re-visit the list and alter it as a couple later if you choose to. REMEMBER that every decision that you make has the best interest of the kids in mind. Even if the end result is to strengthen your marriage, the kids benefit greatly and the family unit becomes stronger as you become stronger as a couple.

Tool: Agree before you begin that if you feel the discussion start to feel like it's becoming heated, either of you can call a time out of 10 minutes or more. Drink a cold glass of water and hug and remind yourselves that this is about improving your home life and making the kids happier.

Taking the time to work through these key issues will greatly increase a couple's odds of success as a couple and will have a profound impact on their family's happiness and well-being.

In the end:

The most important thing to remember is that every decision and agreement that you make should be in the best interest of your kids. When in doubt, use this as a yardstick to help you decide what makes the most sense. You and your spouse might not agree with each other on every issue, but putting the kids at the center of your focus will help you keep a keen eye on the ultimate goal. This will help you to find more common ground and help you to agree more and argue less. The subject matter is highly personal to both of you. She feels strongly about her kids. He feels strongly about the subject matter. At times, you may feel that it's the beginning of an argument. The process can easily start to erode and evolve into personal feelings. It seems like you are both struggling for position. Having the kids at the center of your focus will help remind you that it's not about the adults —and help keep you from being drawn towards an unproductive argument. Keeping the kid's best interest a focus will make the process much less-personal.

Continue this process as you move forward with your new family. When you are discussing matters about the kids, ask each other "What's best for the kid?" This will help you to cut through some of the emotion and get to the root of the answer. It may not always make you popular with the kids but it will assure that you have no regrets in the end.

www.ingramcontent.com/pod-product-compliance
Lightning Source LLC
Chambersburg PA
CBHW050558280326
41933CB00011B/1898

* 9 7 8 0 6 1 5 7 4 7 2 3 1 *